Great Monkey Rescue

Saving the Golden Lion Tamarins

Sandra Markle

Millbrook Press • Minneapolis

For my wonderful critique group: Teddie Aggeles, Susan Banghart, Melissa Buhler, Janet McLaughlin, and Augusta Scattergood

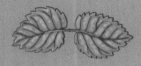

Acknowledgments: The author would like to thank the following people for sharing their enthusiasm and expertise: Dr. Benjamin Beck, Smithsonian Conservation Biology Institute; Dr. Jim Dietz, Save the Golden Lion Tamarin; LouAnn Dietz, Save the Golden Lion Tamarin; Dr. Clinton Jenkins, SavingSpecies; and Dr. Stuart Pimm, SavingSpecies. A special thank-you to Skip Jeffery for his loving support during the creative process.

Millbrook Press
A division of Lerner Publishing Group, Inc.
241 First Avenue North
Minneapolis, MN 55401 USA

For reading levels and more information, look up this title at www.lernerbooks.com.

Main body text set in Metro Office 12/18. Typeface provided by Linotype AG.

Library of Congress Cataloging-in-Publication Data

Markle, Sandra, author.
    The great monkey rescue : saving the golden lion tamarins / Sandra Markle.
        pages cm
    Summary: "A look at the plight of the golden lion tamarin for children."— Provided by publisher.
    Audience: Ages 9–12.
    Audience: Grades 4 to 6.
    ISBN 978-1-4677-8030-8 (lb : alk. paper) — ISBN 978-1-4677-8850-2 (eb pdf)
    I. Golden lion tamarin—Conservation—Juvenile literature. 2. Golden lion tamarin—Reintroduction—Brazil—Juvenile literature.
  3. Habitat conservation—Brazil—Juvenile literature. 4. Corridors (Ecology)—Brazil—Juvenile literature. I. Title.
    QL737.P925M36 2015
    639.97'984—dc23   2014041353

Manufactured in the United States of America
1-44235-34256-5/10/2017

TABLE OF CONTENTS

This female tamarin is eighteen months old. She is ready to mate and have babies.

TRAPPED!

In a small patch of tropical forest, a squirrel-sized golden lion tamarin stops on a high-up branch and listens.

The young female picks out another tamarin's long call. These shrill tweets can be heard over a mile (2 kilometers) away. It's the way a tamarin signals, *I'm here. Is anybody there?*

The young female is searching for a mate with whom she can start a family group. So she goes to investigate.

She finds two family groups together. The youngsters are playing while the mothers nurse their babies. The males chatter and chase one another. Their noises help to claim their family's home territory, the part of the forest where they find food and safe sleeping places. As the young female moves closer, the families stop, get quiet, and stare.

Sometimes a young adult joins a neighbor's family group.

5

Then one female charges and chatters, *Chuck-chuck-chuck!* She is her family's breeding female. Others from both families join in chasing the young female visitor away.

A family group usually accepts and supports only one breeding female.

With her long tail streaming behind her for balance, the young female leaps and flees. Later, she is chased away from another family group she meets in the forest. And the next. No golden lion tamarin family group she finds will accept a new breeding female.

Like all tamarins, this female's tail is much longer than her body.

Clawlike nails help tamarins run along branches and climb high up in trees. Their long fingers help them pick jussara palm fruit.

The young female roams the forest alone. At night she sleeps in any tree hole she can find. That keeps her hidden from sneaky, weasel-like tayras hunting in the tree branches. During the day, she searches for food and stays on the run from the tamarin families whose home territories she crosses. Because whenever she's discovered, she's chased away.

But the young female keeps tracking down the long calls she hears. Then one day, following a new call, she comes to the edge of the forest. Beyond is a grassy field that's bright, hot, and open. So she stays in the forest's cool shadows, sits in a big tree, and listens to the distant tamarin long call.

She's trapped! A prisoner in a patch of forest where no family group wants her. And in this habitat half the size of Manhattan Island, in New York—just 12 square miles (32 sq. km)—there's no territory left to claim.

ALMOST GONE FOREVER

Golden lion tamarins live only in Brazil's Atlantic Forest, in South America. In the past, these monkeys had no problem finding a home territory. This rain forest once stretched all along the country's coastline. So much of this area has been cleared, though, that only a tiny fraction of the forest remains.

The Atlantic Forest once covered the entire area inside the thick yellow outline.

The Atlantic Forest began shrinking long ago, in the 1500s. At that time, Portuguese explorers cut trees to send Brazilian timber back to Europe. Later, some forest areas were cleared for plantations that grew sugarcane, coffee, and other crops. Many of these plantations failed and were then cleared to create cattle pastures. More of the forest was cut down to make way for roads, cities, and towns.

Today, less than 10 percent of Brazil's Atlantic Forest remains. And only parts of that area, along the coast of the Brazilian state Rio de Janeiro, have just the right conditions for golden lion tamarins.

Tree by tree, the tamarins have lost their homes and their food supply.

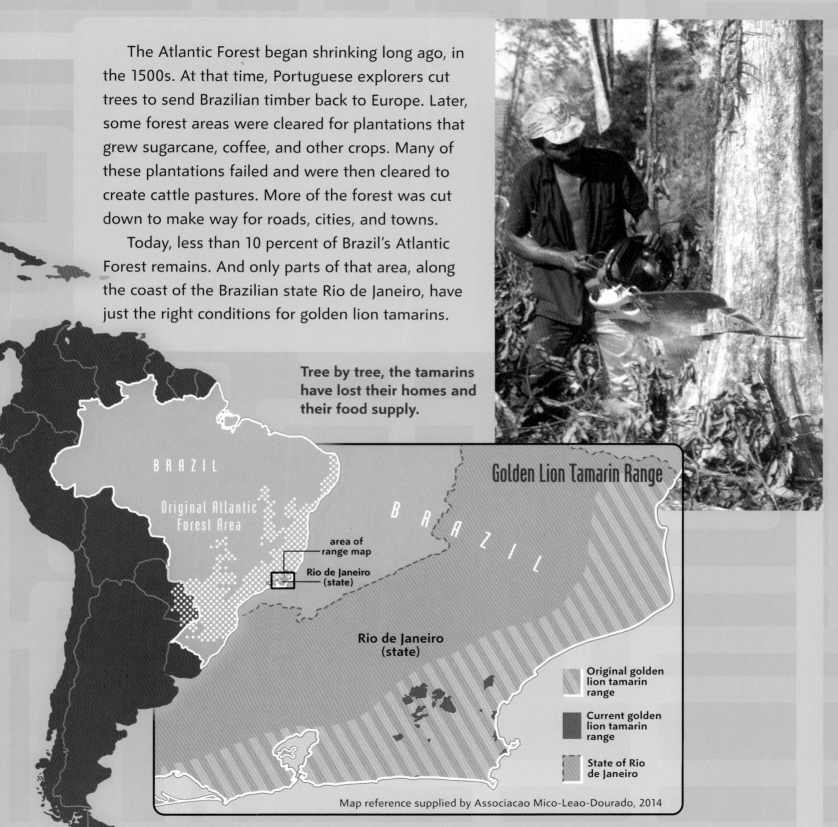

BRAZIL

Original Atlantic Forest Area

area of range map

Rio de Janeiro (state)

Golden Lion Tamarin Range

BRAZIL

Rio de Janeiro (state)

Original golden lion tamarin range

Current golden lion tamarin range

State of Rio de Janeiro

Map reference supplied by Associacao Mico-Leao-Dourado, 2014

11

What Makes the Golden Lion Tamarin's Habitat Special?

Golden lion tamarins make their home in warm, swampy forests with towering trees, whose leafy canopies of branches act like giant umbrellas. The branches shield the monkeys from the hot sun and hide them from flying hunters like ornate hawk-eagles.

The warmth and shade of the forest is perfect for insects, an important food for golden lion tamarins. Many of the trees also produce sweet, pulpy fruits and flowers that tamarins eat.

In addition, bromeliads grow on the trees. These plants catch and hold rainwater, giving the tamarins a place to find a drink midway between the ground and the tree canopies. That's where tamarins spend most of their time, running along the crisscrossing pathways of branches.

Over several hundred years, more and more area of the Atlantic Forest was destroyed. But enough habitat remained for the golden lion tamarins, because the tamarin population was shrinking too. By the early 1960s, scientists estimated only about two hundred remained in the wild. These monkeys were in danger of becoming extinct—gone forever.

Scientists were concerned about losing this unique species (kind of animal). Tamarins play important roles in their habitat. By feeding on insects, they help control populations of bugs that might otherwise harm plants and animals. The tamarins' waste also spreads the seeds of the trees whose fruit they eat, so new trees keep growing. And tamarins are a food source for bigger predators.

A zookeeper at the National Aquarium in Baltimore, Maryland, records a tamarin's weight and follows up with a treat.

Scientists hoped that tamarins in zoos would survive and reproduce to keep the species alive. However, by 1975, that seemed unlikely. At that time, there were only 122 golden lion tamarins living in zoos around the world. Because the monkeys were an endangered species, US zoos had stopped bringing in any more from the wild. And zoo tamarins rarely had babies. Even worse, of the young that were born in zoos, most didn't survive to become adults and have babies of their own. Devra Kleiman, a researcher focused on maintaining healthy animal populations at the National Zoo in Washington, DC, decided that something had to be done to save golden lion tamarins. But what?

Hoping to learn how to help, she led a team of scientists in studying the behavior of the zoo tamarins. They compared their observations to reports on the behavior of wild populations of these monkeys.

The result was a simple but key discovery. Zoos were housing golden lion tamarins in large groups, the way they housed chimpanzees and other kinds of monkeys.

But in the wild, tamarins don't live in big groups. They live in families.

Devra Kleiman checks a tamarin's weight. A healthy adult weighs about 14 to 29 ounces (0.4 to 0.8 kilograms).

All in the Family

Golden lion tamarin families are founded by a mother and father who usually stay together for life and produce babies. The family group may also include one or two males that don't produce young with the female. There may even be a couple of other females that usually don't reproduce. Youngsters stay with the family until they're about eighteen months old or until they're ready to mate.

The key to success for the tamarin family is that everyone helps carry and care for the babies. That's important because each family roams over a home territory as large as 125 acres (51 hectares)—about the size of one hundred football fields! The group needs an area that large to find enough food during the dry periods that happen each year. When the babies stop nursing, everyone helps feed them and teach them what to eat. At night the family finds an empty tree cavity. The babies are put inside this hole first. Then the rest of the family piles on top to keep them warm and safe from prowling predators.

Tamarin babies are usually fraternal twins—babies that are born at the same time but are not identical.

Babies hang on tightly to their parents to stay warm and safe.

Based on what Devra Kleiman's team discovered about these monkeys, the National Zoo changed how golden lion tamarins were housed. The tamarins were separated into pairs, and instead of removing the father once the mother gave birth, the zoo allowed families to stay together.

This worked! Soon the zoo's golden lion tamarins began to regularly produce babies. And those babies survived. The National Zoo shared its success story with zoos around the world. Then the golden lion tamarin population in zoos grew. And it continued growing!

Like all tamarin babies, this youngster grew inside its mother for about four months before birth.

Next, zoos mimicked wild tamarin behavior in another way. The young leave their families or are chased away once they reach breeding age. Then they either join another family group or start one. So the zoos began moving breeding-age animals from one zoo to another. Just as in their native habitat, that kept inherited problems from being passed down within a family group. This especially helped prevent one key problem among tamarins, a physical defect they sometimes develop that makes breathing difficult.

The new breeding program was so successful that by the mid-1980s, there were about five hundred tamarins living in zoos around the world. However, Brazil's wild population was still shrinking. Soon all the remaining wild tamarins would be related and would be more likely to pass on genetic problems. And that could lead to extinction even faster. Something more had to be done.

Zoos kept careful records so relatives did not mate.

BACK TO THE WILD

Scientists decided the answer was to release zoo tamarins into their natural forest homes in Brazil. Ben Beck, a researcher working with the monkeys at the National Zoo, headed up a team of scientists to reintroduce groups of zoo tamarins into Brazil's Atlantic Forest. Zoos around the world agreed to give tamarins to this project.

In all, about fifteen monkeys were chosen to be released in a first attempt in 1984. Some of the selected tamarins were sent directly to Brazil. Others were sent to the National Zoo and joined its reintroduction program. "At the National Zoo," Ben Beck said, "we first wanted to give the tamarins some training on how to live wild and free."

Before being released into the wild, tamarins were measured and examined to be sure they had no parasites (animals that live off other animals), injuries, or diseases they might pass on to wild tamarins.

These tamarins find a bit of fruit tucked under a loose piece of bark. Fruit makes up about 80 percent of the tamarin's diet.

To train the tamarins, zoo caretakers began hiding food in the trees. The monkeys had to poke under bark and look in tree holes to find their meals. Fruit was no longer peeled or cut up. The tamarins had to figure out how to eat what they found. As they would in the real forest, the tamarins also now drank from bowls attached high up on the tree trunks. Zoo workers hoped this training would give the monkeys a better chance of surviving in the wild.

In 1974 the Brazilian government had created the country's first protected area of swampy forest, the Poço das Antas (POH-so das AHN-tas) Biological Reserve. This 19-square-mile (50 sq. km) forest was set aside especially for the golden lion tamarins. So when zoo tamarins were ready to be released in the wild, the reserve was chosen as the first site for the reintroduction program.

Before the release, a radio collar was placed on at least one member of each family group so they could be tracked. Then some groups of tamarins were released directly into the open forest.

The tamarins reintroduced in Brazil learned to bite open the armor-like exoskeletons of insects to eat what was inside.

Radio collars allowed scientists to find tamarin groups wherever they went in their very large territories.

For others, a part of the forest was caged over. This area was screened over to a height of about 10 feet (3 meters), and it covered an area about as big as a single-car garage. For the tamarins released into this area, it was a halfway home—a place between the safety of being tended in a zoo and living free. And these tamarins continued to be trained to seek out food. This time, though, the fruit provided was what was available locally to wild tamarins. And the soon-to-be-wild tamarins sometimes found other food for themselves, such as insects.

Finding enough to eat wasn't the only challenge in the wild. So was staying safe. While traveling around the forest and feeding, tamarin family members regularly call out to stay in touch with one another. They also give an alarm call to let others know if they spot danger, such as a big snake or hunting bird.

But for the zoo tamarins released into the open, their natural fears were not enough to keep them safe. The forest was an alien world to them. They didn't recognize some hunters, like tayras, as dangerous. So some were killed by predators. The tamarins also didn't know about Africanized bees, a type of aggressive bee that lives in colonies in tree cavities. So some tamarins made the mistake of choosing tree holes to sleep in that were already home to Africanized bees. Then those monkeys were killed by beestings.

Tayras try to ambush tamarins in their dens at night.

The biggest problem for the tamarins was finding enough food in the forest that they could safely eat. Some ate poisonous fruit and died. Most simply couldn't find enough food. Within six months, most of the released tamarins had died. The next year, in spite of additional training before release, a second attempt with about a dozen tamarins failed too.

Over the next few years, support after release helped some tamarins survive. But few groups became truly able to make it on their own. "We released them," said Ben Beck, "but we put out food for them. If they got lost, we used their radio collars to find them. If they got hurt or sick, we took them to a vet. We were just running a zoo in the wild."

Something had to change if zoo-born tamarins were going to survive on their own in the forest.

A baby holds on tightly while its parents eat the food put out for them in the forest.

TURNING POINT

By the beginning of the 1990s, the reintroduction effort was big news in Brazil. And Brazilians wanted this beautiful little monkey that was native only to their country to survive. A few people who had wild-born golden lion tamarins as pets gave them up for release. A few more wild-born tamarins that had been captured by poachers (illegal hunters) were recovered by the government. In 1991 six wild-born tamarins joined zoo-born ones being reintroduced into the forest. This made a difference: the tamarins started finding enough to eat. But something else even more important began to happen.

Tamarins had to learn which fruit was poisonous and what was safe to eat, such as these berries.

The surviving zoo-born tamarins began to have babies. The babies thrived and seemed to have instincts for living in the forest that their parents didn't, though scientists didn't understand why. And once those youngsters grew up, they started family groups of their own. Finally, the reintroduced tamarin population was growing!

By the time they're ten weeks old, babies are finding and eating their own food.

GOOD NEWS, BAD NEWS

Scientists barely had time to cheer before the next setback. It was clear that all too soon, the Poço das Antas Biological Reserve would be maxed out on the number of tamarin family groups it could support. In addition, private forests were still being cleared, so tamarins in other locations were also running out of home territories.

However, one remaining section of Atlantic Forest covering 12 square miles (32 sq. km) had no known resident tamarins. And it wasn't privately owned. It belonged to the Federal Railway Network. Brazilian citizens, along with supporters from around the world, went to work. They formed support groups to contact politicians, urging them to make this forest available for the golden lion tamarins.

Most remaining forest patches were privately owned. That meant they could be cleared at any time.

Wild tamarins had no trouble moving to a new home as long as the forest habitat was familiar.

In 1994 forty-three golden lion tamarins whose own territories were about to be cut down were moved to this forest. And in 1998, this area became the União Biological Reserve, Brazil's second protected forest for golden lion tamarins. Scientists monitoring the tamarins saw the population in this new reserve rapidly increase. That was wonderful news! But it was also cause for concern.

Although other patches of forest were not far—one was even within sight of this new reserve—they were like islands, separated by large cattle pastures. And the tamarins wouldn't cross those open spaces to find new territory. So, in time, golden lion tamarin family groups would claim all of this forest too. Then what?

Stuart Pimm and Clinton Jenkins, scientists from the organization SavingSpecies, visited the União Biological Reserve. They walked across the pasture that separated it from another patch of forest where few tamarins lived. "Thinking about the animals trapped in the Reserve gave us an idea," Pimm said. "What if a section of the pasture was planted with trees? Could a living bridge be created between the two forests?"

This was a novel reforestation idea, but they decided it was worth a try. SavingSpecies partnered with other groups to raise enough money to purchase the pasture between the forests from the farmer who owned it. When that finally happened in 2007, the land was turned over to the Brazilian government. Then it was time to think about what trees to plant to create a forest bridge.

Even the forest birds weren't willing to fly across this stretch of pasture to travel from one forest area to another.

Not just any kind of trees would do. The trees in the forest bridge needed to be native species—the kinds of trees that were naturally found in the forests where tamarins live. And they had to be fast-growing, because the tamarin family groups were multiplying and needed new territory. The trees also needed to be able to grow well in full sun. They would be planted on bare land without other, bigger trees to shade them. So Brazilian forest expert Carlos Alvarenga directed volunteers in collecting just the right kinds of tree seeds.

Next, three tree nurseries planted the seeds—each in its own bag of soil. The saplings (young trees) were carefully tended until they were about 2 feet (0.6 m) tall. Then they were ready for planting.

Forty-three different kinds of trees were grown for the forest bridge.

Tree seeds were collected in Poço das Antas and other tamarin home forests.

A WAY OUT

The first trees for the living bridge were planted in 2009. It took a huge amount of work to turn a strip of pasture into a forest area. Tough, hardy grass covered the pasture. So before each sapling could be planted, volunteers first had to use a brush cutter, a sort of chain saw, to clear a 6- by 9-foot (1.8 by 2.7 m) patch of ground. Then they had to dig a hole for each sapling.

Little by little, they planted the beginning of a new forest. At first, it was only a narrow corridor. But they continued to plant until trees covered an area about 1,558 feet (475 m) wide and 3,805 feet (1,160 m) long. For the next three years, volunteers visited regularly to pull weeds and grass sprouts that could choke out the saplings.

A hole 1 foot (0.3 m) deep was dug for each sapling.

And the trees grew. By 2012 the trees were about 10 feet (3 m) tall on average. That's not tall enough to be a tamarin home, but it was big enough for these monkeys to crawl along the branches.

In April 2012, Clinton Jenkins reported, "A group of golden lion tamarins was first seen crossing [the forest bridge]." The idea for a living bridge was paying off—thanks to the effort of countless scientists and tamarin supporters. The project was a success!

The planted land was named Fazenda Dourada—Golden Farm—because it was planted especially for the golden lion tamarins.

HOME AT LAST

The young female golden lion tamarin lingers at the edge of her home forest. She has been turned away by every family group she has met. But across a bright pasture, she again hears a new tamarin's long call. It's coming from another forest nearby. Slowly, she edges along a branch. She sees an area of trees just beyond the giant trees she calls home. These are shorter, and their branches don't yet form the thick cover she is used to. But they provide some shade and a new treetop path to explore. So she leaps.

Golden lion tamarins have sharp vision, excellent hearing, and a keen sense of smell to stay aware of everything going on around them.

Landing on a branch in one of the shorter trees, she races along. Then she leaps again. Her long tail streams behind her for balance as she keeps going from one tree to the next. All the while, the shrill long-call tweets continue. They guide her to a new patch of the Atlantic Forest beyond the corridor of shorter trees. There she finds the caller, a young male tamarin.

The young male is searching for a mate, and the young female joins him. Together they claim part of this forest for their home territory. In time, they will raise babies of their own.

The golden lion tamarin population is now one family group stronger.

In the wild, golden lion tamarins usually mate in June and July (the dry season). Most babies are born during October and November (the rainy season), when there is plenty of food.

A GOLDEN FUTURE?

By 2014 scientists estimated the wild golden lion tamarin population had grown to about 3,200. Scientists believed that number would be enough for this species to continue to survive. That is, as long as more forest areas continue to become protected. More forest bridges also need to be planted for the tamarins to travel between the remaining fragments of native forest.

But tamarins aren't the only animals trapped by shrinking forests. Efforts to restore forests for other animals are going on in countries around the world. The golden lion tamarins' success story is inspiring people to search for even more innovative ways to help animals and the habitats they call home.

Older students help younger ones as school groups raise saplings. These groups are helping to build more forest bridges.

Author's Note

When I first learned about this reforestation project, I knew it was a story I wanted to tell. And each time I interviewed an expert who was involved in the project or was studying golden lion tamarins, my research revealed a bigger story. It compelled me to dig deeper. It also made me more excited to continue researching and writing.

The decadeslong effort to save golden lion tamarins involved one project after another. And with each challenge and success, more people wanted to do their part to help these little monkeys. Best of all, the collective effort paid off. With some creative thinking and public support, scientists found a long-term solution!

This story has a happy ending that's all the better because it's true. And in real life, the story continues. More forest bridges are being planted for golden lion tamarins.

In other parts of the world, reforestation projects are also under way to help other animals. The Bornean orangutan, the pygmy elephant, and the Malayan sun bear are just a few of the world's species that are threatened by losing their natural habitat. But with greater awareness and support for these projects, their outcomes could be as hopeful as the golden lion tamarins'. More happy endings are yet to come.

Did You Know?

Baby tamarins make a loud rasping noise when they want to be fed.

Tamarins have a special alarm call for big predator birds flying overhead. And they seem to be born knowing that call means they should drop from the branches to the ground to escape quickly. Even babies in protected zoo enclosures do that!

Tamarins are active during the day and sleep at night. They spend most nights in different tree holes as they move through their home territory. If they can't find a hole, they'll sleep in a thick tangle of vines.

Tamarins call along the boundaries of their territory to stake their claim to their part of the forest. They also rub against branches with their chests, which have scent glands. They mark territorial boundaries and tree sleeping holes with their scent that way.

Timeline

Here's a quick look at the events that led to a hopeful future for Brazil's wild golden lion tamarins:

1960s Scientists believe only about two hundred wild golden lion tamarins remain.

1966 Because of the endangered status of golden lion tamarins, the American Association of Zoological Parks and Aquariums (later renamed the Association of Zoos and Aquariums) support a ban on importing golden lion tamarins to zoos.

1972 Scientists from around the world meet to talk about how to save golden lion tamarins. Devra Kleiman joins the staff at the National Zoo in Washington, DC.

1974 Poço das Antas (19 square miles, or 50 sq. km) is set aside as the first protected forest in Brazil. It is chosen because it contains a golden lion tamarin habitat.

1975 Only eighty-three golden lion tamarins remain in zoos outside Brazil and thirty-nine in zoos in Brazil. Devra Kleiman seeks ways to improve the tamarin breeding program at the National Zoo in Washington, DC.

1980 Copying successful efforts at the National Zoo, zoos see increases in the number of zoo-born golden lion tamarins worldwide.

1981 Zoos start sharing golden lion tamarins for breeding.

1984 Zoo-born golden lion tamarins are released in Brazil to boost the wild population and prevent relatives from breeding and passing on inherited problems.

1991 The reintroduction program is successful.

1992 The Associação Mico-Leão Dourado (AMLD), a Brazilian nongovernmental organization, is created to study and help wild golden lion tamarins.

1998 The União Biological Reserve (12 square miles, or 32 sq. km) is set aside especially for golden lion tamarins.

2005 Save the Golden Lion Tamarin (SGLT) is started in the United States.

2007 Land is purchased to plant a forest bridge—the Fazenda Dourada (Golden Farm) between two forests that are golden lion tamarin habitats (União Biological Reserve and a private farm).

2009 The first trees are planted for the forest bridge on Fazenda Dourada.

2012 Golden lion tamarins are first seen crossing the forest bridge.

2014 Scientists estimate the wild golden lion tamarin population to be 3,200, enough to sustain survival if the tamarins' forest habitat is preserved.

What is one thing you would like to be able to add to this timeline in the future?

Glossary

bromeliad: a kind of plant found in parts of North America and South America with warm, moist climates. These plants have short stems and stiff, spiny leaves. Some types grow on tree trunks.

family group: a group that lives together and shares carrying and caring for babies produced by one breeding pair. A golden lion tamarin family group usually includes a mother, a father, their offspring, and possibly one or two single males, a single female, or both.

fraternal twins: two babies born at the same time that are not identical—sometimes not even the same sex

habitat: the natural home environment of a plant or animal

poachers: people who hunt animals that are protected or who go where they are not allowed to hunt, especially to capture or kill animals

predator: an animal that hunts and eats other living things in order to live

sapling: a young tree

species: one type of living thing

Find Out More

Check out these books and websites to discover even more:

Arkive Golden Lion Tamarin
http://www.arkive.org/golden-lion-tamarin/leontopithecus-rosalia/videos.html
This series of short videos lets you see tamarins in action and listen to some of the sounds they make. Don't miss seeing them climb trees and catch a large insect to eat.

Golden Lion Tamarins at the Zoo
https://www.youtube.com/watch?v=GocPrkS3iD8
Learn about a golden lion tamarin family at the Palm Beach Zoo and watch them in action.

Langley, Andrew. *Navigators: Rainforests.* New York: Kingfisher, 2010.
Explore the world's rain forests and check out what makes the golden lion tamarin's Atlantic Forest home special.

Save the Golden Lion Tamarins
http://www.savetheliontamarin.org/what-kids-are-doing/
Learn how children around the world are helping golden lion tamarins.

Stewart, Melissa. *New World Monkeys.* Minneapolis: Lerner Publications, 2008.
Compare golden lion tamarins to other monkeys living in Central and South America to find out how each species is unique.

Wildlife Wednesdays: Disney Efforts Help to Protect the Golden Lion Tamarin's Forest Home
https://www.youtube.com/watch?v=m1MkgXOSmFw
Watch this overview of the effort to save the Golden Lion Tamarin.

Zoo Atlanta: Golden Lion Tamarins
http://www.zooatlanta.org/golden_lion_tamarin#oQL37
See videos of these monkeys and watch them in action on the live zoo camera.

LERNER
SOURCE

Expand learning beyond the printed book. Download free, complementary educational resources for this book from our website, www.lerneresource.com.

Index

Photo Acknowledgments

The images in this book are used with the permission of: © Laura Westlund/Independent Picture Service (leaf), p. 11 (map); © Eric Gevaert/Dreamstime.com, p. 1; © Claus Meyer/Minden Pictures/CORBIS, p. 4; © Roving Tortoise Photos, pp. 5, 28; © Mark Bowler/Minden Pictures, p. 6; © Haroldo Palo Jr./NHPA/Photoshot, p. 7; Courtesy of Jim Deitz/www.savetheliontamarin.org, pp. 8, 11 (right), 15, 20, 21 (inset), 23, 24, 26, 33, 34; © Anup Shah/naturepl.com, p. 9; NASA, p. 10; © Tom + Pat Leeson/ardea.com, pp. 12, 19; © George Grall, National Aquarium, p. 13; © Benjamin B. Beck, p. 14; AP Photo/Smithsonian National Zoo/Jessie Cohen, p. 16; AP Photo/Martin Meissner, pp. 17, 36; Jessie Cohen, Smithsonian's National Zoo, p. 18; © John Giustina/Photoshot, p. 21; © Martin Wendler/NHPA/Photoshot, p. 22; © Bill Coster/Minden Pictures, p. 25; © Luciano Candisani/Minden Pictures/CORBIS, p. 27; © Luiz Claudio Marigo/naturepl.com, p. 29 (left); © Frans Lanting/CORBIS, pp. 29 (right), 30; © Photo by Clinton N. Jenkins, Visiting Professor at the Instituto de Pesquisas Ecológicas (IPÊ), Brazil, and Vice President of SavingSpecies, p. 31; © Haroldo Palo Jr./NHPA/Photoshot, p. 32; © Bo Jonsson/Skansen Akvariet, p. 38.

Front cover: © Colombini Medeiros, Fabio/Animals Animals; © Laura Westlund/Independent Picture Service (leaf).

Back cover: Photo by Clinton N. Jenkins, Visiting Professor at the Instituto de Pesquisas Ecológicas (IPÊ), Brazil, and Vice President of SavingSpecies.